I0560596

JAMES

FOR A NEW
GENERATION

RYAN HELLER

JAMES FOR A NEW GENERATION

ISBN: 979-8-9996514-0-2 paperback
ISBN: 979-8-9996514-1-9 ebook

INTRO

WE CAN USUALLY see the counterfeit a mile away. Phony grins. Cheap excuses. Token friendships. We've become extremely good at sniffing out anything just authentic enough to look like the real thing but still feels like nothing. But for some reason, we have a much harder time with fake faith. We seem to accept spiritual practices that leave us feeling empty. We settle for shallow answers that don't really solve the deeper questions. We embrace half-truths that only affirm what we want to hear.

Perhaps part of the reason is we've never seen what real faith actually looks like. That's where James comes in. This was not a scholarly theologian writing from afar about religious debate. James knew the real Jesus. He spent considerable time with Jesus as his half-brother. He saw real faith up close and personal, year after year. James knew the real thing before he believed it. And then, one day, it clicked. Everything changed. When he wrote this letter, he had one purpose: to show people what faith actually looks like in real life.

James for a New Generation is for anyone tired of playing spiritual games. If you are over surface-level Christianity that looks great on Sunday but doesn't last until Tuesday, this is for you. If you long for faith that actually matters in the messy places of being human, James has something to say.

This is not about becoming a better person through sheer willpower or spiritual discipline. This is about how God can change you from the inside out. Transform the way you see. Reshape your priorities. Rewire your reactions to life's inevitable trials. As you spend time in these daily devotions, you will begin to experience:

- Joy that doesn't come from your circumstances but from confidence in God's character.
- Wisdom that comes from hearing God rather than figuring everything out on your own.
- Faith that shows up in the choices you make when no one is watching.
- Maturity that values growth over perfection and authenticity over appearance.

Every day, I will ask you to be real about where you are, not where you think you should be. James doesn't shrink away from any part of life. He addresses how you speak when irritated, how you react when things don't turn out like you want, what you do with anger, and how you treat those who are different. Nothing is off limits.

It's going to be challenging, because James doesn't dish out easy answers or feel-good clichés. He gives us something better: truth that transforms, grace that equips, and hope that never fades.

You don't need perfect faith. You need real faith. You don't need spiritual perfection. You need genuine transformation. You don't need to impress God. You need to know Jesus.

So let's begin. One day, one verse, one honest conversation with God at a time.

Ryan Heller

TABLE OF CONTENTS

1. Joy Hacking

Consider it great joy, my brothers and sisters, whenever you experience trials... James 1:2 (CSB)

WHEN LIFE throws you a curveball, the last thing you want to do is cartwheels. When your car breaks down, your boyfriend/girlfriend dumps you, or your bank account stinks, *great joy* is not the first thing that comes to mind. But James isn't telling us to put on a plastic smile or fake it till we make it. He's not saying, "Look on the bright side of things!"

James is prescribing a joy hack. He's hacking life's trials by revealing the infinite value of suffering. Joy is not a toxic positivity or a desperate denial of pain. Joy is seeing that God is working when we cannot see it. God never wastes your pain. He isn't on Instagram when you're in the trenches. He is at work. In you. He is building you into something beautiful that could never be made without the fire.

The joy that James is talking about is not joy because of your circumstances, but joy because of your confidence that God is working in them. Smile through your tears, not because you are fake, but because you know that the Author of your story is not yet finished with the next chapter.

That's the hack. It is not about escaping life's struggles. It's about outsmarting them. It's the holy cheat code that turns pain into purpose and trials into training. When you know God is using even the messiest of moments to make you more like Jesus, you don't have to wait for joy; you can walk in it.

Live It Out:

- When trials come today, pause and pray, "God, what are you building in me through this?"
- Write a gratitude list naming areas you've been blessed.
- Trade "Why is this happening to me?" for "What is God teaching me through this?"
- Don't suffer alone—find trusted friends and authentically share your struggles (real community is better than Instagram illusion any day).

2. God's Gym

...because you know that the testing of your faith produces endurance. And let endurance do its full effect, so that you may be mature and complete, lacking nothing. James 1: 3-4 (CSB)

NO ONE JOINS A GYM on day one thinking they're going to bench press 300 pounds. You start with smaller weights, do some sets and reps, and work your way up so you can handle the big iron. Your faith is the same way.

Adversity isn't God punishing you; it's His personal trainer. Every trial is a spiritual rep building your faith muscles and making them stronger than before. Let that sink in: Would you get surgery from a surgeon who's never had a complicated case? Would you trust a president who's never had a crisis? Most of the leaders you respect have scars not because they're wounded, but because they've been built up through adversity.

Joseph went from pit to palace. David from shepherd boy to king. Their trials were not detours; they were roads to their destiny. This sounds bizarre, but when you do physical exercise and tear down a muscle, it grows back stronger than before. The same happens with character. The trial that's tearing you down is building you up for tomorrow.

Perseverance isn't just gritting your teeth and surviving; it's allowing God to do His thing until you're mature, complete, and lacking nothing. The Christian life isn't a spa day; it's boot camp. And the end product is worth every rep.

Live It Out:

- Keep a "perseverance journal" where you note how trials have made you stronger.
- Don't shrink from challenges. Ask God for strength to walk through them head-on.
- Celebrate baby steps on your faith journey; every forward move matters.

3. Kneel Before You Navigate

Now if any of you lacks wisdom, he should ask God—who gives to all generously and ungrudgingly—and it will be given to him. But let him ask in faith without doubting. For the doubter is like the surging sea, driven and tossed by the wind. James 1:5-6 (CSB)

YOU'RE DRIVING IN CIRCLES, getting more frustrated by the minute, too proud to ask for directions. That's exactly how we handle life's problems. We try to figure it out ourselves instead of asking the One who literally knows everything. God isn't holding out on you. He's not playing hide-and-seek with the answers you need. He's waiting for you to ask.

God doesn't give wisdom with a side of shame. He doesn't roll His eyes and say, "Seriously? You don't know this by now?" He gives generously without finding fault. That means you can come to Him with your messiest questions, your most embarrassing struggles, your deepest confusion, and He won't judge you. He'll help you.

But it only works if you actually believe. Doubt makes you like a wave: unstable, tossed around by every circumstance, never anchored to anything solid. Faith is your anchor. When you pray with faith, you're not just hoping God might help, you're confident He will.

James knew what he was talking about. They called him "Camel Knees" because he prayed so much he had calluses on his knees. This isn't theory from someone in an ivory tower. This is battle-tested wisdom from someone who lived it.

Live It Out:

- Before checking your phone each morning, ask God for wisdom about one specific decision.
- Before making major choices, spend time in prayer rather than just analyzing pros and cons.
- When you feel overwhelmed, stop and pray instead of spiraling into anxiety.
- Exercise believing prayer. Pray as if you're confident God will answer, not just hoping He might.

4. Crown Goals

Blessed is the one who endures trials, because when he has stood the test he will receive the crown of life that God has promised to those who love him. James 1:12 (CSB)

ATHLETES TRAIN for years to win a trophy that will eventually collect dust on a shelf. They sacrifice, sweat, and push through pain for a moment of glory that fades. But you're playing for something infinitely better—a crown that lasts forever. Every trial you endure with faith, every moment you choose love over bitterness, every time you keep going when you want to quit, God sees it. And He's keeping score.

This isn't about earning your way to heaven; that's already been paid for by Jesus. This is about God recognizing and rewarding faithfulness. It's about the magnificent moment when you'll take that crown He gives you and lay it at Jesus' feet in worship. Your pain has purpose. Your perseverance has a payoff. Your faithfulness has a future reward.

The key phrase here is *those who love him*. You can go through trials and become bitter, or you can go through trials and still love God. The difference isn't in what happens to you, it's in how you respond to what happens to you. When you can say, "God, I don't understand this, but I still love You," that's when you know your faith is real.

This sounds bizarre. Why endure hardship for rewards you can't see? But that's exactly what makes it faith. You're not living for the applause of people who will forget you; you're living for the approval of the One who will never forget.

9

Live It Out:

- Don't quit in the middle of the trial—your crown is on the other side.
- When life hurts, respond with love. Let your trials deepen your relationship with God, not drive you away from Him.
- Keep your eyes on the finish line. One day, you'll lay your crown at Jesus' feet and realize it was all worth it.
- Encourage others who are struggling by reminding them of the eternal perspective.

5. Catfish Christianity

But each person is tempted when he is drawn away and enticed by his own evil desire. James 1:14 (CSB)

YOU'VE BEEN CATFISHED. Someone online pretends to be something they're not, and you fall for it. Temptation works the same way. It's the ultimate catfish. It promises pleasure but delivers pain. It looks like freedom but brings bondage. It seems like you're missing out, but you're actually dodging a bullet.

James uses the word *enticed*, which in Greek literally means "to bait a hook." Temptation never shows up looking dreadful. It doesn't knock on your door wearing a name tag that says, "Hi, I'm here to destroy your life." It shows up looking like exactly what you want, promising exactly what you think you need.

The enemy is a master marketer. He doesn't advertise the hangover, just the party. He doesn't show you the regret, the shame, the consequences that follow. He just dangles that perfectly crafted lure in front of you and whispers, "You deserve it."

Don't forget, you're smarter than the trap. You can see the hook and refuse to take the bait. You recognize the lure for what it really is: a trap meant to destroy you. The key is learning to look beyond the shiny packaging and understand the true cost.

Live It Out:

- When something looks "too good to be true," ask yourself, "What's the hook I'm not seeing?"
- Before making decisions, think through the real consequences, not just the immediate pleasure.
- Learn to recognize your personal "lures." What specific baits are you most likely to bite?
- Remember: if it's pulling you away from God, it's not worth taking the bait.

6. Own Your Mess

But each person is tempted when he is drawn away and enticed by his own evil desire. James 1:14 (CSB)

WE LOVE PLAYING the blame game like it's our favorite sport. "The devil made me do it." "Society is corrupt." "I'm just wired this way." "If my boss wasn't such a jerk..." Sound familiar? We've all been there. James drops a hard truth that makes us deeply uncomfortable: the problem isn't out there; it's in your core. Your heart is the actual crime scene, not the victim.

When you realize that temptation starts with your own desires, you also realize you have more control than you thought. You're not a puppet being controlled by

11

external forces around you. You're not a victim of your experiences. You're a person with real choices, and those choices matter more than your circumstances.

Imagine that temptation is like a God-given desire turned completely wild. Hunger is good; gluttony is destructive. Ambition is healthy; greed is toxic. Intimacy is beautiful; lust is damaging.

The desire itself isn't evil; it becomes harmful when it breaks free from God's protective boundaries. James knew exactly what he was talking about. As Jesus' half-brother, he watched the most tempted man in history never give in to sin. He saw that victory over temptation starts with taking responsibility for your own heart.

You can't control what temptations come your way, but you can absolutely control how you personally respond to them.

Live It Out:

- Stop blaming external factors and take ownership of your choices.
- When tempted, pause and ask, "What desire in my heart is driving this?"
- Pinpoint which God-given desires in your life have gone off the rails.
- Practice daily heart-checks—ask God to reveal what's really motivating you.
- Replace "I can't help it" with "I choose what's right."

7. A Bun in the Oven

Then after desire has conceived, it gives birth to sin, and when sin is fully grown, it gives birth to death. James 1:15 (CSB)

YOU KNOW THAT MOMENT when someone announces they're expecting? Everyone gets excited about the new little bun in the oven. But James uses pregnancy language to describe something terrifying: how sin matures inside us. And unlike a pregnancy, this is one announcement you never want to make: "I'm expecting…trouble."

Sin doesn't just happen. It grows. It starts as a tiny seed of desire, gets fertilized by our choices, and eventually gives birth to consequences we never intended. And just like a pregnancy, once the process starts, it has a life of its own.

Look closely: no one wakes up planning to ruin their marriage overnight. It begins with small compromises, little lies, tiny betrayals. One decision leads to another until suddenly you're left holding the pieces of what once was, asking how it happened.

The scary part? Sin grows in the dark. It thrives in secrecy, feeds on isolation, and multiplies when no one's watching. That "harmless" habit you're hiding? That "small" compromise you're justifying? That "private" thought life you think doesn't matter? James is warning you: it's growing, and it will eventually give birth to something you don't want.

However, there is always hope: you can stop the process at any stage. You can recognize the conception before it becomes full grown. You can confess the desire before it becomes action. You can get help before the consequences become irreversible.

Live It Out:

- Write down three desires that could become sinful if left unchecked, then share one with a trusted friend.
- Shine a light on it. Confess temptations to trusted friends before they grow.
- Ask yourself, "What small compromises am I making that could grow into big problems?"

8. Opening Act

By his own choice, he gave us birth by the word of truth so that we would be a kind of firstfruits of his creatures.   James 1:18 (CSB)

WHAT IF you were the opening act and not the main event?

Let that sink in. Before every great concert, there's an opening act that warms up the crowd for the headliner. That's you. You're not here to get applause. You're here to warm hearts for the main event. When Jesus returns to heal and restore all creation, your life is the preview trailer of God's coming attraction.

James drops this radical truth. Believers aren't God's ultimate masterpiece. We're God's opening act for the greatest concert of celestial history. When God gave you new life by His truth, He made you a preview of how He's going to restore the entire universe.

As firstfruits, you're God's deposit. You're His promise that He's not done with this broken world. When the world sees authentic transformation in your life, it's getting a preview of the cosmic renovation project God has in store. Your healing, joy, integrity, and compassion all foretell of the coming glory.

God didn't make a mistake by making you the opening act. Your life is a holy calling. You're here to set the stage, warm up the crowd, and create expectations for the headliner. Every act of love, moment of integrity, and display of God's character fuels excitement for the main event.

Your life is not about becoming a star. It's about preparing others to meet the real Star when He comes.

Live It Out:

- Embrace your supporting role. When tempted to seek credit or recognition, redirect attention: celebrate others, serve without expecting thanks, and find joy in being part of God's bigger story.
- Explore how you can be a better "preview trailer" for God's ultimate main event. Share with someone how God has transformed your life.
- Invite someone who's been hurt by church to experience God's love through your church family. Be their personal preview of grace.

9. Think Before You Talk

My dear brothers and sisters, understand this: Everyone should be quick to listen, slow to speak, and slow to anger.
James 1:19 (CSB)

IN OUR CULTURE of hot takes, instant reactions, and keyboard warriors, this sounds almost counter-cultural: shut up and listen. We live in a time where everyone has an opinion about everything and we feel the need to share it ASAP. But spiritual maturity isn't about how quickly you can respond; it's about how wisely you choose your words.

The *listen* here isn't passive hearing; it's active, intentional engagement. It's setting aside your own agenda, silencing your internal commentary, and truly seeking to understand not just the words being said, but the heart and emotions behind them. It's the kind of listening that listens to understand, not just to respond.

We are all experts at listening poorly. We are already formulating our comeback while the other person is still talking. We are quick to speak and slow to hear, but James flips the script. He says be *slow to anger* because he knows that when we are quick to speak, we are usually quick to get hot under the collar.

Human anger rarely serves God's purposes. It's more about protecting our ego than pursuing righteousness. But when you're slow to speak, you give yourself time to process, pray, and respond in wisdom rather than react in emotion. This is a spiritual discipline. It's about the maturity to pause before you post, think before you text, and pray before you respond. In a world full of noise, the person who knows when to be quiet is going to stand out.

Live It Out:

- Practice the 24-hour rule: wait a day before responding to emotionally charged messages.
- Focus on understanding the other person's perspective before sharing your own.
- Ask more questions and make fewer statements in your interactions.
- Before posting on social media, ask yourself, "Is this helpful, or am I just venting?"

10. Spiritual Selfie

But be doers of the word and not hearers only, deceiving yourselves. Because if anyone is a hearer of the word and not a doer, he is like someone looking at his own face in a mirror. For he looks at himself, goes away, and immediately forgets what kind of person he was. James 1:22-24 (CSB)

THERE'S ALWAYS THAT PERSON who treats every reflective surface like a runway moment. They're obsessed with their reflection. However, James talks about a different kind of mirror-checking—one that most of us are terrible at. God's Word is like a spiritual mirror that shows us who we really are, but too many of us are just glancers instead of gazers.

A glancer takes a quick look, sees what they want to see, and walks away unchanged. A gazer looks intently, honestly examines what they see, and adjusts. The difference between spiritual maturity and spiritual stagnation is often the difference between glancing and gazing.

Spiritual glancing is extremely common. We skim a verse, listen to a sermon, read a devotional, and think we're good. But James warns that this kind of surface-level engagement is self-deception. You're lying to yourself if you think hearing God's Word without doing it counts for anything.

The mirror of God's Word doesn't lie or distort. Rather, it shows you the truth about who you are and who you can become. But unlike a regular mirror that just shows you what's wrong, God's Word also shows you how to fix it. The question is, are you looking long enough to see what needs to change?

17

Live It Out:

- Spend more time studying fewer verses instead of skimming through large passages.
- After reading Scripture, ask yourself, "What is this showing me about myself that I need to change?"
- Keep a journal of specific ways God's Word is challenging you to grow.
- Meditate on one verse for an entire week. Consistently ruminate on the passage and its message.

11. Game On

But the one who looks intently into the perfect law of freedom and perseveres in it, and is not a forgetful hearer but a doer who works—this person will be blessed in what he does.
James 1:25 (CSB)

WE ARE OBSESSED with life hacks, shortcuts, and fast fixes. Everybody wants the blessing without the work, the reward without the effort, the transformation without the discipline. But James drops a truth bomb. God's blessings aren't unlocked by what you know; they're unlocked by what you do with what you know.

Think about it like a video game. You can watch a million YouTube tutorials, memorize every cheat code, and study every strategy guide, but until you actually pick up the controller and play, you'll never level up. The same is true with your faith. You can attend every church service, listen to countless sermons, and fill your phone with Bible apps, but if you're not putting God's Word into practice, you're still stuck.

James promises that when you become a doer of the Word, you'll experience two game-changing blessings: inner peace and greater freedom. Inner peace comes when you know you're living according to God's design for your life. Greater freedom happens when you realize that God's boundaries aren't restrictions; they're guardrails.

The word *blessed* doesn't mean you'll get rich quick. It means you'll experience God's favor and approval on your life. When storms come (and they will), you'll have the unshakeable foundation of knowing you built your life on God's Word.

Live It Out:

- Pick one biblical command you've been avoiding and actually do it this week.
- Stop consuming more spiritual content until you've applied what you already know.
- Measure spiritual growth by obedience, not just knowledge.

12. Deep Fakes

Pure and undefiled religion before God the Father is this: to look after orphans and widows in their distress and to keep oneself unstained from the world.   *James 1:27 (CSB)*

DEEP FAKES are everywhere. Tom Cruise dancing on TikTok (spoiler: it's not really him). Politicians saying things they never said. AI-generated celebrities hawking products they've never used. Digital deception has become so sophisticated that we can barely trust our own eyes.

But the most dangerous deep fakes aren't digital; they're spiritual. James gives us a simple authenticity test to separate genuine faith from religious performance. Real Christianity shows up in measurable ways through the widows and orphans test.

Do we care for the most vulnerable? James highlights widows and orphans as ancient society's most defenseless members. Today that means foster kids, single parents, elderly neighbors, or anyone society has forgotten.

Here's the gut check: If someone followed you around for a week, would they witness James 1:27 in action? Would they see you caring for the vulnerable without expecting anything in return?

Authentic faith leaves evidence. Your calendar reveals priorities. Your bank statement shows values.

This isn't advanced Christianity; it's baseline faith. If we're not meeting this standard, we need to realign our lives.

Spiritual authenticity is impossible to fake forever. The real you will eventually surface. When it does, will people see genuine love in action or just another deep fake?

Live It Out:

- Anonymously pay lunch debts for kids at a local school or support a foster family with dinner, babysitting, or encouragement.

- Challenge yourself to see "invisible" people—learn your janitor's name, thank your server personally, or encourage someone working behind the scenes.

- Identify one vulnerable person in your community and take concrete action to help them this week.

13. Favoritism Doesn't Fit

My brothers and sisters, do not show favoritism as you hold on to the faith in our glorious Lord Jesus Christ.   James 2:1 (CSB)

BLUE CHECKMARKS, follower counts, viral moments—it's all about who's known, who's trending, who's connected. And if we're not careful, that same obsession creeps into our churches, our friendships, even our theology.

James isn't talking to atheists or outsiders. He's writing to believers. People who claim the name of Jesus but still judge others by how much influence they carry. It's easy to mask favoritism with spiritual language—"I just really feel led to invest in that person"—when really, we're drawn to their platform, not their person.

Favoritism shows up when we're quick to greet the well-dressed guest but barely nod at the one who looks out of place. It happens when we network more than we disciple, when we choose friends based on how they can help us rise instead of how we can help them grow. It elevates certain people while quietly devaluing others. Jesus didn't chase fame; He ran toward the forgotten. He didn't build a brand; He built people.

If Jesus left heaven to embrace the poor, the marginalized, the invisible, how can we claim to follow Him while curating relationships like we're building a PR strategy? Favoritism doesn't fit.

The gospel isn't just good news for the famous. It's hope for the overlooked. It levels the playing field, reminding us that every soul has infinite worth, not because of their résumé but because of their Redeemer.

Here's the truth: if your circle only includes people who elevate your image, you might be following popularity, not Jesus. He didn't die to build a cool crowd; He came to create a community centered around the cross, where the least and the lost are just as loved as the most influential in the room.

Live It Out:

- When planning social events or gatherings, intentionally include people who might not make the "obvious" guest list, especially those who rarely receive invitations.
- Pray for God to give you His lens, one that values hearts over hype.
- In your next church service, sit in a different section and make a point to introduce yourself to someone you don't know, especially someone who seems alone or like a newcomer.

14. Royal Flush

Indeed, if you fulfill the royal law prescribed in the Scripture, Love your neighbor as yourself, you are doing well. If, however, you show favoritism, you commit sin and are convicted by the law as transgressors. James 2:8-9 (CSB)

EVER PLAYED POKER? The royal flush is the best hand in the game—unbeatable, elusive, and worth it all. In the poker game of life, James says there's one royal law that trumps every other rule: *Love your neighbor as yourself.* It's God's royal flush, and when you play this hand, you win every time.

We like to think we can play favorites and still claim we're obeying the King's law. James calls that bluffing. You can't love your neighbor as yourself while treating some neighbors better than others. It's like claiming you have a royal flush when you're really holding a pair of twos. It's not just wrong, it's delusional. The word *royal* here isn't just fancy talk, either. This law comes from the King of kings, which means it outranks every other rule in your personal playbook. Your cultural preferences, your comfort zones, your natural biases all fold when the royal law hits the table. Love doesn't discriminate based on bank accounts, zip codes, Instagram followers, or social status.

James gets brutal about this. If you show favoritism, you're not just being rude, you're breaking God's law. It's like cheating at cards. You might fool the other players for a while, but the house always knows. And in God's house, partiality is a losing hand every time. Love's beauty is this: when you play the royal flush, everyone comes out ahead. The person you love feels cherished. You win by fulfilling your purpose. And God wins because His character is revealed through you.

The question isn't whether you know this law—most people do. The question is whether you're actually playing it. Are you holding the royal flush of love in your hand, or are you still trying to win with a deck full of prejudice and favoritism?

Live It Out:

- Before making judgments about people, ask yourself, "Am I playing the royal law or my personal preferences?"
- Remember, love isn't just a feeling. It's a choice to value others the way God values you.
- Challenge your inner circle: Are you building a clique or building the kingdom?

15. Holding Grudges Holds You Back

For judgment is without mercy to the one who has not shown mercy.
Mercy triumphs over judgment.   James 2:13 (CSB)

LET'S FACE IT. That grudge you're holding against that person—it's not harming them. It's harming you. Way more than you realize.

If you let it go, what exactly do you lose? We think resentment protects us. That it somehow gives us leverage. But unforgiveness is spiritual, emotional, and yes, even physical poison. It creeps into your soul slowly. You tell yourself you're hurting them with it, but all it's really doing is hardening your heart.

Breaking this verse apart is not only teaching us about how God judges; it's a revelation about how we live. If judgment is leading, we're cultivating an inner life full of bitterness, fear, and self-righteousness. If mercy is leading, we enter into the same freedom we're clamoring for.

Judgment is like spiritual junk food. When we do it, we're satisfying something in the moment: our ego, our pain. But it bloats your soul. It makes you sick. It makes you heavy. Mercy is the detox. Mercy is what flushes out the junk. It washes over you like a flood and cleanses your heart. Mercy leaves room for peace.

We often hesitate to extend mercy because we feel like we're not "holding people accountable." But forgiveness is not saying what they did was okay. It's saying, "I refuse to let this dominate me anymore." Mercy is not for the weak. It's the opposite of weak. It's strength. It's spiritual maturity. It's courage. Mercy is choosing to be set free.

24

If you feel like your heart is heavy, your joy is stifled, and peace is hard to find, ask yourself, "Who am I still holding in judgment? What am I still clinging to that God has been asking me to let go?" Start there. Inventory. Name it. And then, even if it's the hardest thing you'll do this year, choose mercy. You're not only setting them free; you're setting yourself free. Because holding grudges may feel like strength, but mercy, that's the real strength. It's the master key to your chains.

Live It Out:

- Make a list of people you're judging or holding grudges against, then choose to release them.
- Practice mercy by giving people the benefit of the doubt instead of assuming the worst.
- When you catch yourself being judgmental, stop and ask, "How would I want to be treated in this situation?"
- Replace critical thoughts about others with prayers for their well-being.

16. Show Me the Receipts

What good is it, my brothers and sisters, if someone claims to have faith but does not have works? Can such faith save him? If a brother or sister is without clothes and lacks daily food and one of you says to them, "Go in peace, stay warm, and be well fed," but you don't give them what the body needs, what good is it?
James 2:14-16 (CSB)

EVERYTHING NEEDS RECEIPTS. No selfies means it didn't happen. No W-2 means you're lying about your job. No Netflix shows means you never streamed them.

25

We live in a receipt world where everything requires verification and documentation.

Spiritually speaking, faith needs receipts too. If you say you have faith but there's no evidence of it in the way that you live, it's possible that you're full of hot air and just playing empty games with God Himself.

Envision this scenario: your neighbor is cold and hungry, and they are standing right in front of you, desperately needing help and looking for compassion. You look at them sympathetically and say, "Bruh, I'm praying for you. God got you. Just stay warm, eat good." Then you stroll away without hesitation, not even giving them your jacket or buying them a meal. James is like, "Bro, for real?" That's not faith. That's heartless behavior disguised as spirituality and righteousness.

Genuine faith has a paper trail. Faith leaves behind concrete receipts. Faith shows up on your bank statement and your calendar and your text messages and your weekend itinerary. If the I.R.S. sent auditors into your life, could they find evidence that you actually believe what you say you believe? Or would they just see a bunch of religious bluster without any proof or substance backing it up whatsoever?

This is the gut punch: James isn't talking to atheists. He's talking to church people. To the people who know all the pious clichés and hashtag all the Bible verses. But when it comes to rolling up their sleeves and helping other people, they're nowhere to be found.

Let James remind you clearly that the demons believe in God too. And they shudder at His name with genuine fear and trembling. See, the demons have receipts for all their belief and commitment. The question is, do you have yours ready to show?

26

Live It Out:

- This week when you encounter someone in need, don't just pray for them, help them.
- Ask yourself, "If someone followed me around for a week, would they see receipts of my faith?" If so, where?
- Start a "faith receipts" journal. Document the ways you put your faith into action every day.

17. All In: The Abraham Test

Wasn't Abraham our father justified by works in offering Isaac his son on the altar? You see that faith was active together with his works, and by works, faith was made complete.
James 2:21-22 (CSB)

ABRAHAM GOT THE ULTIMATE TEST. He had to sacrifice the thing he loved most. God asked him to put his precious miracle son, the one he waited 100 years for, on an altar. Can you imagine the weight of that moment? Most of us would have laughed, cried, or called God crazy. But Abraham packed his bags and headed to the mountain. That's not just faith. That's all-in, no-questions-asked, ride-or-die belief.

Consider the beautiful reality that God didn't want Isaac dead. He wanted Abraham's heart fully alive in trust. The moment wasn't about sacrifice. It was about surrender. It was about discovering what mattered most.

The test revealed something significant: Abraham's faith wasn't just intellectual. It was active. He didn't just believe God could do something; he acted like God would do something. His faith had legs. It moved. It took risks.

27

God tests our faith to build us, not break us down. He's growing us into who He created us to be. Every single time you choose obedience over comfort, trust over control, God's will over your way, your faith gets stronger and deeper. The question isn't whether God will test your faith. He will. The question is, what will the test truly reveal about what you really believe deep down?

What's your Isaac? What's the thing you're holding so tightly that you can't imagine letting it go? Your career? Your relationship? Your reputation? Your comfort zone? God is asking, "Do you love it more than you love me?"

Live It Out:

- Detect what you're holding onto too tightly and practice releasing it to God in prayer.
- When God asks you to step out of your comfort zone, say "yes" before you have all the answers.
- Look for opportunities to choose God's will over your preferences this week.

18. Closer Than You Think

And the Scripture was fulfilled that says, Abraham believed God, and it was credited to him as righteousness, and he was called God's friend. James 2:23 (CSB)

YOU KNOW THOSE MOMENTS when you're looking at the stars (or stuck in traffic) and it suddenly hits you that the same God who made the galaxies actually longs to have coffee with you? It's a crazy thought (and maybe a little arrogant), but that's what we're talking about. God doesn't want to be some distant cosmic Power we occasionally text when life goes wrong—He wants to be our friend. The kind we can argue with about His choices. Just ask Abraham.

What was the best part about Abraham's friendship with God? It was awkward and messy. Think about your very best friend: the one who's seen you at 3 A.M. at your lowest, who knows about that embarrassing high school thing, who you call when you need truth even when it hurts. That was Abraham's relationship with God. When God wanted to wipe out entire cities, He basically said, "Hey Abe, what do you think?" Which isn't how you talk to acquaintances.

Most of us are perfectly fine keeping God in the "helpful but not too involved" category. We want Him close enough to bail us out of our messes, but not so close that He starts asking awkward questions like, "Why are you still mad at that person?" Abraham didn't care about maintaining that distance. He wanted the kind of friendship where God would literally show up for dinner and they could work through the hard stuff in person.

Sometimes I think we've become so accustomed to treating God like a distant cosmic Power that the idea of actual friendship feels...wrong. Maybe too intimate? The messy miracle of Abraham's story is this: you don't have to have your act together to be God's friend. Abraham lied about his wife being his sister (twice!), doubted God's promises, and made terrible parenting choices. But he kept showing up for the friendship. That's what God wants from us—not perfection, but presence.

This same invitation that changed Abraham's life is sitting right there waiting for you. God doesn't want to be your emergency contact. He wants to be the first friend you think to call. The question isn't whether He wants you (spoiler alert: He does). It's whether you're ready to move from knowing about Him to actually knowing Him.

Live It Out:

- This week, share one thing with God you never felt comfortable talking with Him about before. Be vulnerable and transparent.
- Look for opportunities God might be trying to use you in what He's doing. Pray and seek.
- Develop a stronger friendship with God. Think of God as your friend, not just your fixer.
- Practice including God in your ordinary moments. Invite Him into your commute, your lunch break, or your evening routine.

19. High Stakes: Betting Everything

In the same way, wasn't Rahab the prostitute also justified by works in receiving the messengers and sending them out by a different route? James 2:25 (CSB)

RAHAB WAS PLAYING a dangerous game. When the Israeli spies came to her door, she had a choice: hand them over and live safely, or hide them and risk everything. She chose option two and it changed the course of her life. Sometimes faith is betting everything on God when the odds are against you.

Consider Rahab's circumstances: living in enemy territory, working in a shady profession, and now harboring fugitives. If she was found out, it was game over. And yet, something about these men and their God made her take the biggest gamble of all. She believed in their God and acted on that belief in a way that could have cost her everything.

Wow. Rahab went from prostitute to part of Jesus' family tree. She married into the Jewish nation, had children, and became the great-great-grandmother of King David. One act of faith rewrote her entire legacy. That's what happens when you trust God instead of playing it safe.

Most of us are risk-averse when it comes to faith. We want guarantees, safety nets, and backup plans. But faith by definition means uncertainty. If you could see the outcome, you wouldn't need faith. God calls us to step out when we can't see the whole staircase, to move when we don't know the destination, to trust when we don't understand the plan.

The wonderful thing about betting on God is that even when you lose everything else, you win what matters most. Rahab lost her old life but gained a new identity. She lost her security but gained God's protection. She lost her reputation but gained a place in history.

Live It Out:

- Recognize one area where God is calling you to take a risk and stop making excuses.
- When facing a decision, ask yourself, "What would I do if I knew God would come through?"
- Build your faith muscles by taking small acts of risky obedience.
- Trust that God's track record is better than your backup plan.

31

20. Zombie Faith

For just as the body without the spirit is dead, so also faith without works is dead. James 2:26 (CSB)

THE WALKING DEAD look alive from a distance, but up close, you realize there's no life in them. They're just going through the motions, stumbling around without purpose or power. James says that's exactly what faith looks like when it's not accompanied by action—it's zombie faith.

Zombie faith shows up to church, knows all the right words, and can quote Scripture like a pro. It looks religious from the outside, but there's no spiritual pulse. It's faith that's technically alive but functionally dead.

The scary part about a deadhead faith is that you can have it for years without realizing it. You're going through all the religious motions (praying, reading your Bible, attending services), but your life isn't actually changing. Your character isn't improving. Your relationships aren't getting healthier. You're spiritually flatlined.

James uses a brutal comparison: a body without a spirit is a corpse. Faith without works is the same thing: spiritually dead. You can dress up a corpse, put makeup on it, and prop it up, but it's still dead. You can dress up dead faith with religious activity, but it's still powerless to transform your life.

But here's hope: zombie faith can be resurrected. The moment you start putting your faith into action by helping people, making sacrifices, taking risks for God, your faith comes back to life. It gets a pulse. It starts breathing. It becomes the living, active, transformative force God designed it to be.

Live It Out:

- Write down three specific areas where you know God wants you to grow—maybe it's forgiveness, generosity, or patience. Choose the one that scares you most because that's probably where you need breakthrough the most. Within the next 48 hours, take one concrete action step in that area.

- Stop consuming more spiritual content until you've applied what you already know. Your faith does not need more information; it needs more implementation.

- Make *faith without works is dead* your daily mantra and use it as a spiritual pulse check. Ask yourself each evening, "What did my faith actually do today beyond existing in my head?"

21. Mighty Mouth

So too, though the tongue is a small part of the body, it boasts great things. Consider how a small fire sets ablaze a large forest.
James 3:5 (CSB)

ONE MATCH can burn down a whole forest. A small leak can sink a great ship. One tiny virus can shut down the whole world. In the right circumstances, the littlest things have the biggest impact, and your tongue is no exception.

It's only a few inches long, but it has the power to build empires or destroy lives with just a few words. James likens your tongue to a horse's bit and a ship's rudder—both small pieces of equipment that control something much bigger. A bit might weigh a pound, but it can steer a 1,200-pound horse. A rudder is a tiny fraction of a ship's size, but it determines where the whole vessel goes. Your tongue is the same. It's small but steers your whole life.

Think about the words that have impacted you. Someone might have said, "You're brilliant," and your confidence took off. Or someone might have said, "You'll never amount to anything," and you're still fighting that lie decades later. Words don't just vanish into thin air. They lodge in hearts and minds, and they create realities that can last for decades.

The truth is crazy: the power of life and death is in your mouth. Every conversation, text, post is a choice. Will you be a life-giver or a dream-killer? What are you doing with that power? Are you using your tongue to ignite fires of encouragement and hope, or are you burning down relationships and reputations? Your tongue might be small, but it has a massive impact.

Live It Out:
- Ask yourself before you speak, "Will these words build up or tear down?"
- Name someone you know who could use some encouragement and make a point to speak life into their situation.
- Practice the 24-hour rule for emotionally charged texts and messages: wait a day before you hit send.
- Use your tongue as a tool. Make sure you're using it for building up, not for tearing down.

34

22. The Beast You Can't Control

...but no one can tame the tongue. It is a restless evil, full of deadly poison. With the tongue we bless our Lord and Father, and with it we curse people who are made in God's likeness.
James 3:8-9 (CSB)

HUMANS HAVE FIGURED out how to train killer whales to do backflips, teach parrots to talk, and get lions to jump through hoops. We've domesticated wolves into lap dogs and turned wild horses into gentle riding companions. There are even hippos that have learned to roll over like a dog. But there's one beast we've never been able to tame: our own tongue.

James drops this uncomfortable reality: your tongue is more difficult to tame than any animal on the planet. It's unpredictable, dangerous, and impossible to fully control through willpower alone. One minute you're singing worship songs, and the next minute you're tearing someone apart with your words. Same mouth, same tongue, completely different outcomes.

The word *restless* here means it never stops moving, never settles down, never finds peace. Your tongue is like a caged animal that's constantly pacing, looking for an opportunity to break free and cause damage. It's *full of deadly poison*—the same word used for snake venom. That means your words don't just hurt people; they can actually kill their spirit, their dreams, their hope.

Sadly, we use the same mouth to worship God on Sunday that we use to destroy people on Monday. We sing and pray, then gossip in the parking lot. We pray for God's blessing and then curse the driver who cut us off. James basically says, "This is insane. You can't have it both ways."

35

The good news? While you can't tame your tongue through human effort, God can transform it through His power. When your heart changes, your mouth follows. When the Holy Spirit controls your life, He controls your speech. The tongue that was once a weapon becomes a tool for healing.

Live It Out:

- Confess to God the ways your tongue has been "untamed" and ask for His help.
- Ask someone close to you to lovingly call you out when your words are destructive.
- Speak blessings over people instead of criticism or complaints.
- God can transform your heart, but you can't tame your tongue.

23. Code Red

But if you have bitter envy and selfish ambition in your heart, don't boast and deny the truth. Such wisdom does not come down from above but is earthly, unspiritual, demonic. James 3:14-15 (CSB)

THIS IS A CODE RED SITUATION, and not the kind where you slap duct tape on and pray it fixes itself. Your words are not the problem. Your words are the smoke alarm. Jealousy. Bitterness. Selfish ambition. These are not bugs in your heart's operating system. They are destructive malware woven into your heart's source code. James isn't mincing words here: *bitter envy* and *selfish ambition* are not moral weaknesses. They are *demonic*.

When jealousy is your guide and selfish ambition is your conversation fuel, you're not just having a bad day.

You're on the Enemy's software. The wisdom that originates from hell is earthly, unspiritual and demonic, and it will crash your mouth every time.

We have all tried the band-aid solutions: "Just speak more positively." "Use affirmations." "Say it in love." But trying to filter your words without filtering your heart is like putting a filter on a cracked lens. The distortion will leak right through. If the source code of your heart is infected with demonic jealousy and ambition, the message you send will be infected, no matter how nice it sounds.

Your mouth is not broken. It is reflecting. When your heart is full of peace, words of encouragement come easily. When it's full of pride, defensiveness comes easily. When it's infected with bitter envy, complaints and criticism come easily. Your mouth speaks what your heart has been stewing on.

It's easier to deal with the symptoms, to work on sounding nicer or more spiritual. But that's like putting a bandage on a hard drive crash. The problem is not your presentation. It is your data.

Heart surgery is the only real fix. And heart surgery is always painful. But that's where healing starts. It's time to let God take out the jealousy you've labeled "ambition," the bitterness you've labeled "discernment," the pride you've labeled "confidence."

When God cleanses the heart, the tongue becomes self-healing. You won't have to battle for better words when your heart is full of better motives.

Live It Out:

- Ask God to search your heart and remove any jealousy or selfish ambition you might have.

- Fight the spiritual warfare necessary to defeat envy and ambition in prayer and Scripture.
- Trade jealous thoughts for gratitude. Trade selfish ambition for God's purposes.

24. Single-Source

But the wisdom from above is first pure, then peace-loving, gentle, compliant, full of mercy and good fruits, unwavering, without pretense. James 3:17 (CSB)

EVERY DECISION you make is energized by something. Some people are driven by fear, others by ambition, approval, or comparison. But James opens his description of godly wisdom with a nonnegotiable: purity. That's not random. It's foundational.

Godly wisdom begins with clean motives. It isn't just about staying away from temptation, it's about aligning the why behind what you do. Purity starts in the heart. A pure heart doesn't mean a perfect heart. It means your intentions are honest, your direction is sincere, and your desire is to please God more than people.

We can fool others with charisma, but we can't fool God with our motives. A person can speak spiritual language, make wise-sounding choices, and still be operating out of selfish ambition, pride, or image management. That's not pure energy. That's manipulation with a spiritual filter.

When your motives are pure, your actions change. You stop chasing applause and start pursuing purpose. You stop trying to build your own name and start serving in Jesus' name. This is what single-source living looks like: one clear motivation instead of mixed signals from your heart. The wise person is not just making good decisions. They are making decisions for the right reasons.

Purity clears the fog. It gives clarity. It brings peace. It helps you hear the voice of God instead of the noise of the crowd. Jesus lived this way. His motives were never mixed. Every word, every move, every miracle came from a heart fully aligned with the Father.

Ask yourself, "Why am I really doing this?" That question can change everything. It helps filter out pride and pressure. It brings your soul back to center. It keeps you grounded in the kind of wisdom that doesn't need to prove anything because it is rooted in truth.

Live It Out:

- Evaluate your motives in one area where you are prone to impress or perform. Make appropriate changes.
- Let go of one habit or relationship that keeps pulling your motives in the wrong direction.
- Pray Psalm 51:10: *God, create a clean heart for me and renew a steadfast spirit within me.*
- Before acting, ask, "Why am I really doing this?" Let God speak to your motives.

25. Reason > Reaction

But the wisdom from above is first pure, then peace-loving, gentle, compliant, full of mercy and good fruits, unwavering, without pretense. James 3:17 (CSB)

MOST OF US are one bad email, one slow driver, or one passive-aggressive text away from blowing a gasket. But when many lead with outrage and impulse, what would it look like to live with reason over reaction?

James says that godly wisdom is compliant or open to reason. In the Greek, the word implies a willingness to yield, to listen, to not assume you know everything. It's the posture of humility: being teachable, flexible, not just defending your point.

That's a radical concept in a world of canceling, clapping back, and curating echo chambers. We've been conditioned to see changing our minds as weakness and listening as losing. But James flips the script: being open to reason is actually a mark of spiritual maturity.

The reasonable person isn't spineless or indecisive. They're just secure enough in God's wisdom to listen before they speak and slow their reaction so they can hear the Holy Spirit. They understand that being right isn't as important as being wise.

Jesus modeled this perfectly. Even under pressure, He asked questions. He listened. When the Pharisees tried to trap Him, He didn't react defensively. He responded thoughtfully. His decisions were rooted in reason, not just emotion or convenience.

Consider the difference. Reaction comes from self-protection and assumes the worst. Response comes from security and seeks to understand. Reaction shuts down conversation; response opens it up.

Being reasonable doesn't mean you'll always agree with others, but it does mean you won't instantly dismiss them. It means you'll pause, pray, and weigh your decisions through the lens of wisdom, not just what you feel in the moment.

Choosing reason over reaction is countercultural. But when you respond with thoughtful wisdom instead of emotional reactivity, you create space for real dialogue.

Live It Out:

- Before making a tough call or sending that text, ask, "Am I reacting emotionally, or responding reasonably?"
- In one conversation today, practice active listening: don't interrupt, don't assume.
- When someone disagrees with you this week, respond with curiosity, "Help me understand your perspective."
- Pray, "God, make me open to reason, slow to speak, quick to hear, and willing to grow. Help me choose wisdom over winning."

26. Fruit Over Flash

But the wisdom from above is first pure, then peace-loving, gentle, compliant, full of mercy and good fruits, unwavering, without pretense. James 3:17 (CSB)

THERE'S A DIFFERENCE between looking good and doing good. That might sound obvious, but optics often outrank outcomes. James gives us a powerful reminder: wisdom from above is full of mercy and good fruits. Not showy. Not shallow. Just consistent, Spirit-led impact.

When something is full of fruit, it doesn't need to perform. It grows quietly and steadily, nourished by deep roots. That's the kind of life God is building in you. Not flashy. Not performative. Faithful. Fruitful.

Jesus taught that good trees bear good fruit. That's not just about behavior; it's about the source. Fruit comes from the inside out. It is evidence of something deeper and healthier than what filters can fake or influencers can fabricate.

41

A wise life will be rich in mercy, not just rich in likes. It will overflow with compassion, not curated content. When we operate out of godly wisdom, we stop trying to impress people and start trying to impact people.

Anyone can go viral for a moment. Not everyone can bear fruit over a lifetime. The call is not to sparkle. It is to serve. The invitation is not to impress. It is to produce something that lasts.

God's wisdom creates a different kind of legacy. One that is full of mercy and full of impact. You may never trend online. You might not be spotlighted. But your life can still be full of fruit that changes other people's lives.

Live It Out:
- Ask God to help you value character over visibility.
- Take inventory of what your life is producing. Are you bearing good fruit or just staying busy?
- Choose service over spotlight in one situation this week.
- Remember that fruit takes time. Stay faithful, even when it feels slow.

27. The Heart Hack

What is the source of wars and fights among you? Don't they come from your passions that wage war within you? James 4:1 (CSB)

EVER FEEL LIKE there's a war zone in your heart? You want one thing yet get pulled in different directions, sometimes fighting with others, sometimes fighting yourself. James doesn't mince words. The reason behind fights and quarrels isn't just circumstances or other people; it's the desires that fight within us.

The game-changer: the gospel is the master heart hack. It rewires our brains, emotions, and responses. It doesn't just bandage conflict symptoms; it transforms the source. When Jesus enters our story, He implants a new operating system into our hearts. The King of Glory descended because our hearts need rescuing.

Before the gospel rewires our hearts, we run on scarcity mode. It feels like there's never enough, so we fight and claw for what we think we need. That's the mentality behind conflicts, jealousy, and selfish ambition. The gospel says "You are enough. You are loved. You are fully known." When we know that truth, our cravings change.

What's the power of the gospel? Your heart doesn't have to fight, compete, or compare with others. It's a heart that knows God's full sufficiency. That peace rewires your reaction to people and circumstances. Rather than lashing out or fighting over status, recognition, or control, you live out grace and generosity.

The good news is that Jesus wires you for this daily as you trust in Him. It's daily surrender—a reset where you invite Jesus to sit with you, scan your heart, and replace your desires with His. That's why James keeps us bringing ourselves into submission to God and resisting the devil because this is how the gospel fights for your heart.

If you're weary from the inner battles and conflicts with others, remember this: the gospel is more than good news; it's powerful, transformative news. It rewires. It renews. It restores.

Live It Out:

- Pause today and notice what desires are waging war in your heart. Pray and ask Jesus to rewire them completely.
- When triggered, remember God's sufficiency for you.
- Meditate on this truth: you are fully loved and accepted.

28. Cheat Codes

You adulterous people! Don't you know that friendship with the world is hostility toward God? James 4:4 (CSB)

NOTHING DESTROYS relationships faster than cheating. The lies. The betrayal. The heartbreak when everything crashes down. That's what James says we're doing when we try being best friends with both God and the world. We're spiritual cheaters.

James isn't using *adulterous* lightly. Throughout Scripture, our relationship with God is described as a marriage: close, exclusive, and faithful. We are bound to God in love. But when we become friendly with the world's values, priorities, and approval, we're cheating on God. We're taking what belongs only to God (love, loyalty, devotion) and giving it to the world.

The world is a smooth talker. It promises acceptance if we compromise a little, success if we bend the rules, or happiness if we chase what everyone else wants. But the truth is, the world's friendship comes with a price tag that will bankrupt your soul.

This isn't about never having non-Christian friends or spending all your time in church. This is about where your heart and loyalties lie. When the world says "fit in," does your heart respond "stick out"? When culture says, "Look out for number one," does your spirit whisper, "Give more"?

James uses the word *hostility*. It's more than disagreement. It's direct opposition to God. When we choose to befriend the world, we're declaring ourselves against God. That's not a casual relationship status. That's a declaration of war.

But here's beautiful news: God isn't trying to ruin your fun. He's trying to rescue you from a death trap. The world's friendship is like a toxic relationship that steals your joy, peace, and purpose. God's friendship provides what this world never can: unconditional love, unshakeable identity, and hope.

It's a binary choice. You're either a friend of the world or a friend of God. "It's complicated" isn't an acceptable relationship status with God.

The good news? The best Friend ever is waiting for you.

Live It Out:

- Break up with toxic influences: Are there relationships, habits, or media that are pulling you away from God? Break up with them.
- Choose your crowd. Choose to hang around people who inspire you to be more like Jesus, not less.
- Daily loyalty check: Ask yourself before making decisions, "Will this choice make me more of a friend to God or the world?"

29. You Don't Have to Hustle

But he gives greater grace. Therefore he says: God resists the proud but gives grace to the humble.   James 4:6 (CSB)

SOME OF US grew up thinking we had to earn love. Be impressive. Be good enough. Stay strong. Don't mess up. That mindset doesn't die easy, and it often sneaks into how we think about God. Maybe if I clean up, pray harder, fix myself...then He'll bless me. Then I'll be close.

But James reveals a different truth. Grace doesn't come to those who have it all together. Grace comes to the humble.

Humility isn't weakness; it's honesty. It's realizing you don't need to fake strength when Jesus already offers rescue. God doesn't hand out trophies for performance. He gives greater grace, the kind that meets you in the cracks and fills what hustle never could.

The gospel isn't: "Try harder, be better." It's: "You couldn't, so Jesus did." And when that truth sinks in, something shifts. You stop sprinting for approval and start resting in love. That's where new life begins, not with a hustle but with a surrender.

So if you feel burned out, buried in pressure, or just tired of trying to impress God, stop running. He's not asking you to climb a ladder or prove your worth through endless effort. He's asking you to come close. He gives grace to the humble. And that changes everything.

Live It Out:

- Encourage someone who's struggling to measure up. Remind them that grace runs deeper than effort.
- Ask the Spirit to show you one way to live like someone who's already loved, not someone still trying to earn it.
- Start your day by reading a gospel passage before checking your phone or email.

30. Why Giving Up Wins

Therefore, submit to God. Resist the devil, and he will flee from you. James 4:7 *(CSB)*

SURRENDER HAS A BAD REPUTATION. We associate it with weakness, defeat, and failure. But when it comes to God, surrender is actually the ultimate power move. It's the white flag that signals victory, not defeat.

Every area of your life where you're struggling is probably an area where you're still trying to be the boss. Your finances, your relationships, your career, your future: you're white-knuckling your way through life, trying to control outcomes that were never yours to control in the first place. And it's exhausting.

James connects submission to God with resistance to the devil for a reason. When you're submitted to God's authority, you automatically have authority over the enemy. It's like plugging into the right power source. When you're running on God's power instead of your own, you have access to strength you never knew existed.

47

Don't mistake submission for weakness. It's not about letting people walk all over you or giving up your personality. God isn't out to ruin your joy. He's directing it. Submission is like a river guided by its banks: not confined, but empowered.

The beautiful irony is that when you stop trying to control everything, you actually gain more control than you ever had. When you submit your plans to God, He gives you better plans. When you submit your will to His will, you discover that His will is actually what you wanted all along. You just didn't know it yet.

Submission is scary because it requires trust. You have to believe that God is good, that He's wise, and that He has your best interests at heart. But once you experience the peace that comes from letting God be God, you'll wonder why you fought so hard to stay in the driver's seat of a life you were never meant to drive alone.

Live It Out:

- Surrender one area where you've been fighting for control.
- When you feel overwhelmed, remind yourself, "God is in control and I don't have to be."
- Start each day by submitting your plans and agenda to God's will.

31. Fight Back: You Have Authority

Resist the devil, and he will flee from you.   James 4:7 (CSB)

THE DEVIL isn't looking for a fair fight. He's looking for easy targets: people who don't know their authority, who don't understand their power, who think they're helpless victims in a spiritual war. But James reveals a powerful truth: you have the power to make the enemy run.

The word *resist* here is a military term that means to take a stand against an advancing army. It's not passive; it's active, intentional, and aggressive. You're not just hoping the devil will leave you alone, you're actively pushing back against his schemes and making him retreat.

It's not a maybe; it's a certainty. *Resist the devil, and he will flee.* That's the power of knowing who you are in Christ. The enemy doesn't get a vote when you stand in that kind of authority.

But resistance requires recognition. You have to be able to identify when the enemy is attacking. That voice telling you you're worthless? That's not God. The temptation to give up on your marriage? That's not wisdom. The overwhelming anxiety about your future? That's not from heaven. Learning to recognize the enemy's voice is the first step in resisting his influence.

The devil's greatest weapon isn't temptation; it's deception. He wants you to believe you're powerless, that you're stuck, that you have no choice but to give in. But the truth is, you have more authority than you realize. When you're submitted to God, you have access to the same power that raised Jesus from the dead.

Fighting back doesn't mean you'll never face spiritual attacks. It means you don't have to be a victim of them. You can stand your ground, speak truth over lies, and watch the enemy flee like the coward he really is. Victory isn't just possible; it's promised to those who resist with faith and determination. This battle was won before it began, and you have everything you need to walk in that victory today.

Live It Out:

- Recognize God's voice versus the voice of the evil one.
- Speak Scripture when facing temptation or spiritual assault.
- Practice saying "no" to the devil's lies and "yes" to God's truth.
- Surround yourself with worship music and prayer when you feel under attack.

32. The Two-Way Street

Draw near to God, and he will draw near to you.
James 4:8 (CSB)

RELATIONSHIPS ARE A TWO-WAY STREET, and your relationship with God is no exception. James drops this sweet truth: God doesn't just want you to be running after Him. He wants to be running after you, too. When you take a step to go toward God, He will take a step to go toward you. When you move to be near to Him, He moves to be near to you.

This isn't about earning God's love or scheming God into blessing you. This is relationship. If you think about your best friendships, they work because they are a two-way street, because both people invest, both people pursue, both people show up. Your relationship with God works the same way. The closer you get, the more you discover about His character, His heart, and His plans for your life.

Draw near is to come toward with intention and purpose. It is not accidentally encountering God or thinking about God when you're in trouble. It's a deliberate act of prioritizing time with Him, pursuing His presence, and making Him the center of your attention. This means creating space in your schedule, opening your Bible with expectation, and approaching prayer as a conversation rather than a wish list.

The amazing truth is that God is already coming toward you. He's not waiting for you to clean up or get to some spiritual level. He's coming after you with wide open arms, looking for any indication you will draw near. His movement toward you brings peace to your anxiety, wisdom to your confusion, and strength to your weakness.

But nearness is intentional. You don't accidentally drift closer to God any more than you accidentally drift closer to your spouse or best friend. Nearness happens when you choose it, pursue it, and make it a priority over other things.

The promise is simple but profound. Your effort won't be wasted. Every prayer you pray, every verse you read, every moment you spend seeking God's presence: He is responding. He is matching your energy. He is reciprocating your pursuit. He is coming near you as you are coming near to Him.

Live It Out:

- Carve out specific time each day to intentionally draw near to God in prayer and Scripture.
- Take the first step when you feel far from God, don't wait for Him to chase you.
- Talk to God all the time. He is with you.
- Remove distractions that keep you from God during your time with Him.

33. Clean Slate

... Cleanse your hands, sinners, and purify your hearts, you double-minded. Be miserable and mourn and weep. Let your laughter be turned to mourning and your joy to gloom. Humble yourselves before the Lord, and he will exalt you.
James 4:8-10 (CSB)

SOMETIMES YOU NEED more than a quick rinse—you need a deep clean. James isn't talking about surface-level improvements or minor adjustments. He's talking about the kind of spiritual detox that gets into every corner of your life and cleans out the mess you've been hiding.

The language here sounds harsh, but it's actually hopeful. James is saying that real change is possible, but it requires real honesty about where you are. You can't clean what you won't acknowledge is dirty. You can't heal what you won't admit is broken. The mourning and weeping aren't punishment, they're the beginning of healing.

Double-minded means you're trying to live in two worlds at once. You want God's blessings but not His boundaries. You want His grace but not His guidance. You want to follow Jesus but also follow your own desires. James says this internal conflict is making you spiritually sick, and the only cure is to choose one master.

The beautiful promise hidden in this tough passage is in verse 10: *Humble yourselves before the Lord, and he will exalt you.* When you get low enough to admit your need for help, God lifts you higher than you could ever lift yourself. When you stop trying to promote yourself and start letting God promote you, amazing things happen.

It's about getting honest enough with God that real transformation can happen. It's about trading your dirty rags for His clean clothes, your limited strength for His unlimited power.

Live It Out:

- Write down one area where you've been trying to serve two masters, then confess it to God and one trusted friend this week.
- Stop trying to clean up your act before coming to God. Come messy and let Him do the cleaning.
- Identify areas where you've been trying to serve two masters and choose God's way.
- Stay humble by admitting mistakes instead of making excuses.

34. The Invisible Trap

So it is sin to know the good and yet not do it. James 4:17 (CSB)

WE ALL KNOW the obvious sins: murder, adultery, stealing. They're loud and hard to miss. But what about the sin of omission? You know what God is calling you to do. You just choose not to. Silence. Look away. Hit snooze.

It's not the big, splashy kind of sin. You won't see it trending on social media. It's quiet. Subtle. It's not what you do but what you don't. And it chips away at trust, relationships, integrity, and character slowly but surely. It's all the good you know to do but choose not to: the text you don't send, the apology you don't give, the injustice you don't confront, the encouragement you don't offer. Sometimes silence speaks loudest of all.

Why is omission such a dangerous trap? Because it feels easy. Doing nothing doesn't make waves, doesn't rock the boat, and doesn't inconvenience people around you. Or so you tell yourself. "No big deal." "Someone else will definitely handle it." But here's the thing: when you choose not to do good, you're allowing bad to stay or grow.

The gospel doesn't just rescue you from sins you commit. It calls you to a life of intentional love and action. Knowing good but not doing it wastes precious opportunities to live like Jesus and be His hands and feet in a world that desperately needs it.

This verse challenges you to examine your "invisible" sins carefully. Are there things you know you should do but won't? People you should encourage but don't? Times when you should act but look the other way instead?

The good news is you can always start doing good. The gospel empowers you to go from knowing to doing. From passivity to purpose. It changes your heart. Strengthens your will. Enables you to overcome inertia completely.

Living out the good you know is never easy. But it's always worth it. When you choose to act, you display Jesus' love and live your faith to the fullest.

Live It Out:

- Think of one specific situation where you've failed to do good and pray earnestly for courage to act.
- Ask God to reveal the "invisible" sins of omission in your daily life.
- Remember: Faith that's truly alive and vibrant always moves from simply knowing to actually doing well.

35. Hurry Up and Wait

Therefore, brothers and sisters, be patient until the Lord's coming. See how the farmer waits for the precious fruit of the earth and is patient with it until it receives the early and the late rains.
James 5:7 (CSB)

MY GRANDFATHER HAD A FAVORITE EXPRESSION he would say to me every time I got antsy waiting on something. "Hurry up and wait," he would say with that twinkle in his eye. He was trying to tell me that you can't make any process better by trying to make things happen sooner. The phrase was an oxymoron when I was a kid, but today I get what he was talking about.

James paints the picture of a farmer to communicate this very same eternal truth. The farmer must "hurry up and wait" every day of his life. He hurries to plow and seed the field and plant his crop. And then he waits on the early and late rains to do what only God can do.

The farmer can't "hurry up" the seasons or cause it to rain out of season. He knows there is a season and a God-given rhythm of growth that man's toil can't speed or control. Trying to harvest early will only spoil the crop; waiting patiently will yield a plentiful harvest.

We live in a society that has forgotten this ancient lesson. We want crockpot results in microwave minutes instead of patient hours. We want immediate gratification in a world that requires endurance and waiting. We want God to answer our prayers today, even when He has designed them to answer through seasons of growth. But spiritual maturity, like agricultural harvest, requires both labor and waiting.

The "hurry up" part is our diligent obedience through prayer, Scripture reading, service, and righteousness.

55

The "wait" part is our trusting of God's perfect timing even when it doesn't line up with our timetable. Both are absolutely necessary for fruitfulness.

My grandfather knew what James is teaching: You can't speed up God's schedule without sabotaging the process. God's delays are not denials.

Live It Out:
- Relax. Stop trying to rush God.
- Hurry to do what God has clearly called you to do today in prayer, Scripture, and service.
- Trust that God is at work, even when it's not evident.

36. The Sacred Art of Waiting Well

You also must be patient. Strengthen your hearts, because the Lord's coming is near. James 5:8 (CSB)

MY GRANDFATHER'S PHRASE "hurry up and wait" wasn't just a lesson in timing; it was a lesson in attitude. He understood waiting isn't passive resignation; it's an active decision to trust the process even when you can't control the outcome. James echoes that wisdom when he instructs us to *strengthen your hearts* while we wait.

Waiting is the easy part. Waiting well is harder. Waiting well requires intentionally fortifying our hearts against the discouragement, doubt, and impatience that naturally creep in during seasons of delay.

Think about how we wait in the doctor's office. We fidget, we check our phones, we complain about the slow service. But then think about waiting for Christmas morning as a kid. We giddily decorated cookies, built puzzles, and watched cheesy Christmas movies over and over because we knew something incredible was coming.

James reminds us *the Lord's coming is near.* That eternal perspective changes our waiting from grumpy endurance into joyful anticipation. We aren't waiting for nothing. We're waiting for Someone. Every delay, every unanswered prayer, every season of waiting is leading us to the moment when that attitude unravels at the return of Christ who makes all things right.

Strengthen your hearts means filling our minds with God's promises, surrounding ourselves with encouraging community, and choosing gratitude over grumbling. It means remembering God's timing is always perfect, even when it didn't feel that way in the moment.

My grandfather knew you can't hurry anything better by trying to force things out of turn. But you can make the waiting better by choosing the right attitude. When we establish our hearts in God's faithfulness, waiting becomes worship.

Live It Out:

- Develop three specific actions to take when impatience strikes during waiting seasons.

- Read God's promises daily. Choose one favorite Scripture promise and meditate on it each morning this week.

- Pray for others in difficulty. Shift focus from your own waiting by interceding for someone else's struggles.

- Practice gratitude journaling. Write down one thing you're grateful for each day, even during frustrating delays.

37. Complaint-Free Zones

Brothers and sisters, do not complain about one another, so that you will not be judged. Look, the Judge stands at the door!
James 5:9 (CSB)

LET'S BE REAL: complaining about people is like a reflex. Maybe it's that coworker who always shows up late or a friend who never texts back. We all do it. But James gives us a dose of reality. When you're constantly throwing shade or griping about others, you're putting yourself on God's radar...and His judgment is coming sooner than you think. Time to hit pause on the complaints.

James 5:9 calls out complaining as more than just harmless venting; it's a serious warning. God, *the Judge*, *stands at the door,* ready to step in and hold us accountable. Complaining about others fractures the community and can breed bitterness, making us forget that we're all part of God's family.

This isn't about ignoring issues or pretending everything's perfect. It's about how we handle frustration. Complaining often feels like relief, but it can quickly turn toxic—dividing rather than uniting. James reminds us that when we grumble against others, we act as if we're above them, but God sees it all.

Living in a "complaint-free zone" means choosing to guard our words and attitudes. It means swapping criticism for grace and impatience for understanding. Preparing for the Judge means building up others, not tearing them down. It's about reflecting Christ in how we talk and treat one another every day.

Live It Out:

- Scan your speech: Take a moment today to notice how often you complain about others. Ask God to reveal attitudes or words that need to change.
- Shut down the gossip loop. The next time someone starts to complain or gossip, choose to redirect the conversation or shut it down with grace. Don't just avoid negativity; be a voice that protects unity and calls others higher.

38. Keep It 100

Above all, my brothers and sisters, don't swear—not by heaven or by earth or by anything else. Don't make your "yes" be "no," and your "no" be "yes," so you don't fall under judgment.
James 5:12 (CSB)

YOUR WORD is either your bond or your betrayal; there's no middle ground. From exaggerated texts to promises made "just because," there's a growing hunger for authenticity. Social media platforms feed us a constant diet of overstatement and empty pledges, where everything is "amazing," promises are made for likes, and commitments are tossed around casually without thought or intention. James zeroes in on this in his letter. He's saying to keep your word. Don't twist your "yes" into a "no," or your "no" into a "yes." Be clear. Be honest. Be real.

Why does this matter so much? Because your word is more than sounds floating in the air around us. It's a reflection of your character, your faith, and your relationship with God. When you say something, you're staking your reputation on it. But when you waver or flip-flop, it chips away at trust, both with others and with God. Every broken promise becomes a crack in your credibility, weakening the foundation of your relationships.

The gospel flips the script on how we use our words. Jesus invites us into a freedom where we don't have to swear by heaven, earth, or anything else to be believed. Our "yes" is yes, and our "no" is no, simply because our character is anchored in Him. That's power. No need for exaggeration, elaborate oaths, or fake promises to make people believe you.

This kind of honesty is rare. It's countercultural. In a world that often rewards hype, overpromising, and spin, living with integrity in your speech sets you apart. It invites others to trust you and ultimately points them to a God who is utterly trustworthy. People notice when someone consistently follows through on their word.

So what does this look like day-to-day in real life? It means saying "no" when you really mean no, without guilt or pressure from others. It means honoring your commitments, even when it's inconvenient or costly. It means being someone people can consistently count on, someone whose word carries genuine weight and matters.

When your "yes" is yes and your "no" is no, you're not just avoiding judgment. You're living out the gospel in a way people can see, experience, and believe in daily interactions with you.

Live It Out:

- Pay attention this week to how often your "yes" matches your "no." Ask God to help you be consistent.

- Practice saying "no" honestly when you need to, trusting God to handle the fallout.
- Follow through on at least one promise you've been tempted to ignore or delay.

39. The Confession Cure

Therefore, confess your sins to one another and pray for one another, so that you may be healed. The prayer of a righteous person is very powerful in its effect. James 5:16 (CSB)

YOU CAN FILTER your face, edit your posts, and script your story, but none of that leads to healing. What James says here cuts through the noise: real freedom starts where you stop pretending. Confession isn't weakness; it's the first step to breakthrough.

James doesn't say, "Keep your struggles to yourself," or "just pray silently and move on." He says, *"Confess your sins to one another and pray for one another, so that you may be healed."* That's not just physical healing, though it can include that. It's also emotional, spiritual, and relational healing. And it starts with honesty.

Confession isn't about spilling all your secrets to everyone. It's about finding trusted, Spirit-filled people and creating space for accountability, prayer, and healing. We weren't designed to carry sin, shame, or secrets in isolation. When we confess, we pull sin out of the shadows and into the light where grace can actually get to it.

The second part of the verse reminds us that prayer is powerful when it comes from someone walking closely with God. It's not about being perfect. It's about being right with God—humble, repentant, and open. That's the kind of life that fuels powerful prayer. When confession and prayer come together in community, chains break and healing begins.

Live It Out:
- Be Bold: Ask God to show you one trusted person you can open up to.
- Don't let fear or pride keep you stuck. Confession isn't about shame; it's about stepping into freedom.
- Pray Powerfully: Don't just listen to others' struggles; pray with them, right then and there.

40. The Elijah Effect

Elijah was a human being as we are, and he prayed earnestly that it would not rain, and for three years and six months it did not rain on the land. Then he prayed again, and the sky gave rain and the land produced its fruit. James 5:17-18 (CSB)

JAMES USES ELIJAH as his prime example of powerful prayer, but notice what he specifically emphasizes: Elijah was a human being as we are. This isn't about a superhuman prophet with special access to God. This is about an ordinary person who learned to pray with extraordinary patience and persistence.

Elijah's remarkable story reveals the deep connection between patience and prayer. He prayed for drought, then waited three-and-a-half years for God's perfect timing to bring rain. During that extended period, Elijah didn't give up on prayer or lose faith in God's sovereign plan. He understood that some prayers require seasons of patient waiting before we see the answer.

Think about the incredible patience required in Elijah's difficult situation. He prayed for no rain, and then had to courageously live through the consequences of that prayer: famine, drought, and national crisis. Yet he faithfully maintained his faith and continued praying, knowing that the same God who could withhold rain could also send it when the time was right.

This is the powerful "Elijah Effect": ordinary people developing extraordinary patience through persistent prayer. Elijah teaches us that some of God's greatest works unfold over extended periods of time. The important key is maintaining our consistent prayer life during the waiting seasons, not just at the beginning and end of our requests.

Elijah's patience wasn't passive resignation; it was active faith expressed through continued prayer. He didn't pray once and forget about it. He remained consistently engaged with God throughout the entire process. When it was finally time for rain, he was ready to pray again with the same fervor and intensity as before. The encouragement for us today is profound: if Elijah, a human being as we are, could develop this kind of patient persistence in prayer, so can we.

Live It Out:

- Decide to pray about this situation daily for the next month, regardless of immediate results.
- Keep your prayers passionate and engaged, not routine or halfhearted during the waiting.
- Stay ready for God's answer. Like Elijah praying for rain after the drought, be prepared to pray with the same fervor when God's timing arrives.

41. The Drought and the Downpour

Elijah was a human being as we are, and he prayed earnestly that it would not rain, and for three years and six months it did not rain on the land. Then he prayed again, and the sky gave rain and the land produced its fruit.   *James 5:17-18 (CSB)*

ELIJAH'S PRAYER LIFE teaches us something profound about God's timing: sometimes the answer to our prayers creates a season of waiting for our next prayer to be answered. Elijah prayed for drought, and God answered immediately. But then came three-and-a-half-years of waiting before he could pray for rain.

Imagine the weight of that waiting. Elijah watched crops fail, rivers dry up, and people suffer—all as a result of his own prayer. Yet he didn't panic or try to reverse course prematurely. He understood that God's timing includes both the drought and the downpour, both the withholding and the releasing.

This reveals a crucial truth about prayer and patience: God's answers often unfold in seasons, not moments. The drought wasn't a mistake or delay; it was part of God's perfect plan to demonstrate His power and call His people back to faithfulness. Elijah had to trust that the same God who could stop the rain could also send it when the time was right.

How often do we pray for something, receive it, and then grow impatient with the consequences or the next phase of God's plan? We want the promotion but complain about the increased responsibility. We pray for opportunities but struggle with the challenges they bring. We ask for growth but resist the uncomfortable stretching process.

Elijah shows us how to navigate these seasons with faith. He didn't spend three years second-guessing his original prayer or demanding that God speed up the timeline. He waited with confidence, knowing that the God who controls the weather also controls the timing.

The drought prepared the way for the downpour. Sometimes God's delays aren't denials; they are preparations for something greater than we originally imagined.

Live It Out:

- Reframe your perspective: Ask God to help you see this season as preparation rather than punishment.
- Thank God each morning for both the current "drought" and the coming "downpour."
- Stop second-guessing: Resist the urge to question God's timing or your original prayer request.

42. Firebrand Prayers

Elijah was a human being as we are, and he prayed earnestly that it would not rain, and for three years and six months it did not rain on the land.   James 5:17 (CSB)

IMAGINE IF YOUR PRAYERS came with a temperature gauge. Would they register as lukewarm, room temperature, or blazing hot? Elijah's prayers would have melted the thermometer—and that's exactly why they moved heaven and earth.

The word *earnestly* in this passage literally means "with sincere and intense conviction." Elijah didn't offer casual, halfhearted prayers; he prayed with the kind of passion that moves heaven and changes earth.

James emphasizes that Elijah was a human being as we are precisely because we might think his powerful prayers were due to some special spiritual status. But the secret wasn't in Elijah's perfection; it was in his passion. He prayed like he meant it, like everything depended on it, because in his heart he knew it did.

Fervent prayer isn't about volume or emotion for its own sake. It's about praying from a heart that's fully engaged, completely convinced of God's power, and desperately dependent on His intervention. It's the difference between reciting a grocery list and pleading for someone's life.

When we pray with fire, several things happen. First, our own faith is strengthened as we express our complete dependence on God. Second, we align our hearts with God's purposes rather than just presenting our wishes. Third, we demonstrate the kind of trust that God delights to honor with His power.

The challenge for many of us is that we've settled for lukewarm prayers. We pray out of duty rather than desperation, routine rather than relationship. We've forgotten that prayer is meant to be a passionate conversation with the God who holds all power in His hands.

Elijah's fervent prayers didn't just change the weather; they changed history. When we pray with that same fire, that same intensity of faith and dependence, we position ourselves to see God move in ways that seem impossible to our natural minds. Do you have the fire?

Live It Out:

- Examine your prayer temperature: Honestly assess whether your prayers have become routine or halfhearted.
- Pray with desperate dependence. Approach God like everything depends on His intervention, because it does.
- Expect God to move. Watch for ways your fervent prayers begin to change both your circumstances and your faith.

43. Life Saver

Let that person know that whoever turns a sinner from the error of his way will save his soul from death and cover a multitude of sins. James 5:20 (CSB)

LIFEGUARDS DON'T RESCUE PEOPLE by jumping in the water and becoming the life preserver. They throw the actual life preserver to drowning people. This verse reveals that God has positioned you as a spiritual lifeguard, but Jesus is the life preserver. Your job isn't to be someone's savior; it's to point them to the Savior.

The person described here isn't some random unbeliever. It's probably someone who's been hanging around church thinking they're good with God, but in reality, they're not. Maybe they know all the right answers, but their heart never actually changed. Maybe they prayed a prayer once but never really gave Jesus control of their life. When you help someone realize they're still spiritually dead despite going through religious motions, you're setting them up to cry out to the real Savior.

Here's what *cover a multitude of sins* actually means: when you help someone see their true spiritual condition, you're helping them figure out what sins they need to confess. You're not racking up forgiveness points or adding to what Jesus already did. You're just being God's tool to help people recognize their mess so they can call on Jesus, who's the only one who can truly forgive and change them.

This kind of spiritual lifeguarding takes guts because you might have to tell church people they're not right with God. You might have to mess with someone's fake confidence. But when someone realizes they actually need Jesus for the first time, that's when real change happens.

Think about the people in your circle right now. Some of them might be drowning spiritually while looking perfectly fine on the surface. They post Bible verses, but their life doesn't match. They show up to church, but leave unchanged. God has placed you in their path, not by accident but on purpose. He wants to use your voice, your story, your courage to throw them the life preserver of truth.

Live It Out:

- Pray for one specific person who's drifting from God and ask Him for an opportunity to speak into their life this week.
- Share your own story of how Jesus rescued you with someone who needs to hear it.
- Step into that uncomfortable conversation you've been avoiding because someone's eternity might depend on it.

Wrapping Up

YOU MADE IT.

That alone says something. It means you didn't just skim the surface—you showed up, day after day, to wrestle with real truth. You leaned in when it got personal. You stayed with it when the challenges hit close to home. And through it all, James has been pulling you toward something deeper: a faith that's rooted, tested, and ready for real life.

This journey through James wasn't about quick fixes or spiritual shortcuts. It was about developing a faith that holds up in the chaos, not just the quiet moments. A faith that knows how to speak life, stand firm, and stay humble. It's the kind of faith that doesn't crack under pressure or collapse in private. It grows. It matures. It shows up different tomorrow because of what you learned today.

But this doesn't stop here.

What happens next is what really matters. Because James isn't the kind of book you just read; he's the kind of voice that follows you. Into your group chats. Into your classrooms. Into your family drama. Into every decision where you'll have to choose: will I live what I believe, or just talk about it?

The world doesn't need louder opinions or prettier posts. It needs people who live what they believe. Who confess when they mess up. Who stand up for others. Who love without an agenda. That's who you're becoming.

So keep going.

Keep pressing in when faith feels inconvenient. Keep praying when you feel like giving up. Keep walking with Jesus even when no one else understands why. Don't worry about having it all figured out. Just don't fake it. Stay honest. Stay hungry. Stay grounded in truth. You've seen that real faith isn't just possible, it's powerful. And it's already at work in you.

Let James continue to speak into your life. Revisit the hard verses. Return to the prayers that hit deep. Let this book be a mirror, a challenge, and a reminder: your faith matters, and how you live it matters even more.

You're not done.

This is just the beginning of something stronger. Let's keep going—one verse, one day, one choice at a time.

FOR MORE RESOURCES FROM RYAN HELLER GO TO

SERMONSIDEKICK.COM
RYANHELLER.ORG

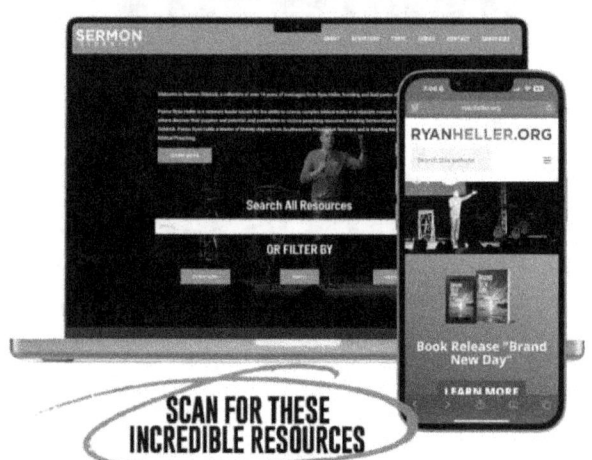

SCAN FOR THESE INCREDIBLE RESOURCES

www.ingramcontent.com/pod-product-compliance
Lightning Source LLC
Chambersburg PA
CBHW071344130626
46556CB00005B/2020